To ERYNN

MN Zoo 2012 Event

Blessings

If only there was...

Another *Summer*

by Cindy Marks

illustrated by Steve Pickar

TiaraMoon Publishing
St. Paul, Minnesota

ISBN 0-9655425-0-5

Library of Congress Catalog Number: 96-90887

Printed in the United States of America.
03 02 01 00 99 5 4 3 2 1

For information address:

TiaraMoon Publishing
3907 Canter Glen Drive
St. Paul, Minnesota 55123

In loving memory of our dear fathers,

Walter Froelich
and
John Pickar

Acknowledgments

Mike and Ryan for your strength,
joy, hugs and laughter. C.M.

Debbie, Jason, Andy & Kyle for your
sunshine every day. S.P.

Dee and LaVina, two dear Moms that give
constant warmth and encouragement.
You are our heroines.

Family and friends for your caring love
and support. Thanks for the stability!

Jack Caravela at Mori Studio for his
creative hand at designing the book
layout and cover.

Pat Morris, as the Compleat Editor, guiding
me through yet another great adventure.
The world of editing.

"This time, like all times,
is a very good one,
if we but know what
to do with it."

— Ralph Waldo Emerson

Contents

If only there was...

Another *Summer*

1 Another Summer

Sitting in the classroom on the first day of school I waited for the school bell to ring. But I hoped it wouldn't.

I stared at the clock and wondered, "How can summer be over already?" I, Cornelius, or Corny as I'm called by my friends, had planned to do much more this past summer. Abby, my sister, had even wished for more time before this dreaded first day of school.

"If only there was another summer," I sighed. There would be no wide eyes staring at the clock. No ringing from the school bell.

There would be no pencils, notebooks, or bad science films about bugs. "Those films are so gross. No one likes to watch slimy bugs crawl on leaves for a whole half hour. At least I don't."

Complete quiet would fill the hallways. Not

12345678910

a shriek or a laugh or even a sneeze. In fact, nothing. No three pages of homework due on Tuesday. No spelling tests on Friday.

If there was another summer, the gymnasium floor would be spotless. Not one black skid mark. All the balls, jump ropes and weights would be packed in the storeroom. Square dancing would be extinct.

Oxenview Elementary could just wait awhile. Until we, Abby and I, decided to start school again. Mr. Elbow, the principal, might get a little lonely by himself. The morning announcements would be short. Nothing to announce.

Ms. Marcias, our Spanish teacher, would have the language room perfectly decorated. A donkey piñata with bright colors would be hanging from the middle of the ceiling. Spanish numbers would be written on the white board.

"Uno, dos, tres" for one, two and three. Not a number, letter or "Welcome Back" sign out of place in the room. Desks, with bold printed names taped square on their tops would be without occupants.

The music room would have no band players with off key voices or instruments. Sam, my best friend, wouldn't squeak when he sang. Mrs. Cherub, the music teacher, wouldn't be there to listen. The music room would be silent.

Most important, our janitor, Mr. Davis, wouldn't have to clean the bathrooms or sweep food off the floor of the lunchroom. What a relief. Some boys and girls are awful messy at lunchtime.

Mrs. Jackson, the school librarian, wouldn't have to say, "Quiet boys, no trading cards in this area." There would be no whispers or tiny giggles getting anyone in trouble. And the bus drivers could all stay home.

2 Pirate Bay Sandbar

We could play at the water park every day with our friends, if there was another summer.

My friend Sam and I would get up early. We'd hop on our bicycles and head to the water park. My sister Abby, too. Once at the park, she'd probably find some trouble. "Slow down, no running," the lifeguard would shout to her.

While Sam was sliding at Swirling Waterfall Canyon, I'd be jumping off the dock at Pirate Bay Sandbar. The water might get in my nose. Pinching my nose tight with my fingers, I would squint my eyes toward the sun and bravely splash into the water. No belly flops. This time not a drop of water would get into my mouth. I hoped.

When we got too hot and thirsty, we could

rest at the Tropical Cove diner. A Beach Creamy drink with a fancy little umbrella and straw would be perfect. An enormous tree would fully block the sun and cool our faces.

If it rained while we were at the water park we might pretend it was a big tropical storm at sea. Pirating would be just the fix for pouring rain. After all, pirates pirate in all kinds of weather. Sam could be the captain of the ship and I the first mate. Abby, of course, could swab the deck.

There might be a mutiny, the crew crying out in pain. Sunburn. All of us pirates would know what to expect next.

Taking turns with the admiral of the pirate fleet, each of us would face our fear but remain calm as Dad wiped loads of gooey cream on each of our faces.

Never again would any pirate, facing a warm summer day, forget the most important supply. Sunscreen.

UDDER
CREAM

YAK
DAVIS
MARTY
BULL

3 Rainy Day Blues

Even a rainy day would be a good day if there was another summer.

Sam and I could play trading cards for hours. We wouldn't even notice the rain. I'd trade my Yak Davis for his Marty Bull card. For hours we'd debate about who's the best baseball player. "Gus Ratkey runs like a bus," Sam would cry.

"Well, Chunk Gipper couldn't throw a ball to his dog if he had to!" Sam and I would argue about all the players; the best, the worst and who just plain stunk. Torn pieces of paper would be scattered on the floor as we made our lists of who to draft. Coach Corny. I think it sounds like a future career.

Even Abby keeps busy on a summer rainy day. She has enough pieces in her Feline Farm

Family Pack to set up a whole town in her bedroom.

Sometimes she makes me help build houses out of cardboard boxes. She calls those boxes "the ballroom with the veranda." I think they just look like boxes with one side flap down and holes cut out of the top. But if it makes her happy, I don't mind. I guess.

Playing games is fun to do when it rains. But if I play with Abby it always ends with her telling on me. Gosh, I'm just kidding around. I don't really cheat. That much.

Abby's fun to play with until she starts to tattle on me. "I'm telling Daddy..." She'd almost sing that phrase over and over again. I like it when her friend Beatrice comes to play. They stay in her room for hours and out of my hair.

SASSY'S SILAGE
WITH GRAVY
YOU BRING THE MILK
MILK
NEW
MILE

EAT
MOO
FOOD
UDDERLY GOOD
FAST
FAST FOOD
FOR COWS ON THE MOOOOVE!

4 Driving Out West

If there was another summer, our family could take a trip. We'd drive out west to spend time in the great outdoors.

Dad would call it the "unspoiled part of the country!" First stop, the mountains. Driving so high we could see snow caps on top of the peaks. Dad would probably let us stop to play in the snow.

Maybe we could build a snowman and make snow angels. Mom would probably play, too. She loves angels. I might even have to throw a snowball or two at Abby. It wouldn't hurt. Would it?

The cabin we'd stay at would be called rustic. I think that's a fancy word for a really old place that smells funny.

Mom would miss not plugging in curlers for her hair. It's kind of scary to think what

Mom would look like without her hair curled.

Lanterns would light the cabin at night. We'd all sit by a campfire and eat Marshmallow Delights with melted chocolate. Abby, of course, would eat too many.

Then late in the evening the "real" fun would start. Ghost stories would be told until they got so scary Abby would start to cry as she moaned, "That poor sweet bunny, he didn't have a chance in the woods with that Giant Scary Thing flying around. No wonder he couldn't get away."

Abby really takes ghost stories too serious. That's okay; it's best to quit the storytelling before Dad starts his stories. Even Mom gets sweaty palms hearing Dad's scary tales. I'm pretty sure it's his deep voice. He doesn't even need to make any monster sound effects. He just talks regular.

5 Grandma Bessie

Grandma Bessie would come with us on our trip. The trip would last for weeks and Grandma would spoil us with too many hugs and kisses.

Every day of our trip, after lunch, Grandma Bessie, Abby and I would walk four blocks to the candy store near our cabin. Grandma would let us pick out two samples of any kind of candy.

Abby would always pick the butterscotch hard candy and Yappy Pappy bubble gum.

I'd choose something different every day. I might pick sour gummy worms and Gobbie Top jaw breakers. When Abby and I eat sour gummy candies our faces twist and scrunch into strange shapes. It's almost like we have to sneeze.

Each night before we went to bed Grandma Bessie would tell us a story about our Grandpa Bovine.

She would whisper our favorite story. "We got married in a tiny church one Sunday afternoon. Grandpa barely made it back to the railroad yard. The nightly run to Millersville almost had to be cancelled that evening."

Another of Grandma's favorites is the story about when Grandpa ran in the Big Deer Race when he was just a young pup. Her smile widens every time she tells it. "Grandpa was just like you, Cornelius, strong and ready to run. That small deer just wasn't fast enough." The whole town cheered when Grandpa won the race.

Grandpa even got his name in the local paper. The town diner, Fast Chew, even named a dinner meal after Grandpa. It was called Quick Quiche Bovine and it came with a 1/2 cup of soup. Made with fresh bouillon, of course.

Maybe, for just one night, Grandma could

START

tell us about Grandpa until the sun came up the next morning. I wonder if I could stay awake that long. I sure would like to try. I know Grandma could talk that long.

Hearing about Grandpa almost makes it seem like he's still around. He spent a lot of time talking with his best friend, Mr. Cattail, at the hardware store when he was younger, Grandma told us. Mr. Cattail is still around but he kind of mumbles when he talks. All I know is when I ask him about Grandpa he gets a grin on his face. "He'd cheat, any chance he could get," Mr. Cattail mutters.

Can cheating run in a family? Next time I get caught, I'll blame Grandpa.

Someday, maybe Sam will tell stories about when we were young. Listening to Grandma sure makes you think about that kind of stuff.

6 The Great Mt. Rushmoo

The best part of our driving trip out west would be stopping to see the Great Mount Rushmoo.

Abby would get sick if we went to see the faces up close in a helicopter. Mom might get a little sick to her stomach, too. Going up to the top of the mountains is okay but looking down from way up there is not.

Worrying that the pilot would get too close to the side of the mountain, Mom would whisper, "I can see his nose hairs too well; this is close enough." Her voice would be a little shaky.

Without checking we'd all be pretty sure that her palms would be sticky and sweaty. Poor Mom doesn't like high places. Roller coasters aren't even an option.

Dad, of course, just enjoyed seeing another

great tourist exhibit with the family. We would get another "When I was young" travel story from Dad. No one minded. By that time, back on the road, Abby would probably be asleep in the back seat. Her favorite doll, Mr. Cowababy, would be crushed to her side.

What a wonderful second summer it would be. More of our Grandma Bessie, more water parks and much more sunshine. Playing pirates at sea and visiting places far away like the Great Mount Rushmoo would fill our days and nights. If I could do it all again, I sure would.

7 Under the Lights

Another summer would be filled with one more final baseball game of the season, played under the evening lights. The score, seven to zero, would be a dream come true.

My Dad would stop at a gas station to ask for directions to the ball field. Better yet, Mom could drive the van. Getting lost before the big game should be impossible.

Abby's doll, Mr. Cowababy, wouldn't get his tail stuck in the door of the van and Mom wouldn't use five bandages. After all, Mr. Cowababy is a stuffed animal.

Our undefeated Oxenview team would play with no errors. The bleachers would be filled with dozens of screaming fans and friends. Buckets of sweat would drip from otherwise perfectly dry parents sitting in the bleachers. Their nervous calls of "It's okay"

S
Ǝ
M
N

and "Good try" after each batter up would echo in the warm night air.

My base line hit to third would be a grand slam home run. No bugs would buzz around my face to weaken my concentration. Absolutely no mosquitoes allowed on the field.

Pitching the last inning, I would shut down the other team's chance of winning. Sam would be at home plate catching my fast ball which stung like fire when it hit his mitt. One, two, three, strike! The evening would be an All Star Game to remember.

When the game was over, it really wouldn't make any difference who won. Once the teams headed for Lucky Antelope's Ice Cream Palace not a word would be spoken about the game.

Poor batting averages and missed catches would be forgotten. There's nothing like a Fudge Twisted Caramel Moose Cone to help you cheer up. Even Hank would forget about striking out. Of course, chocolate can cheer up anybody. We'd all celebrate another fun season.

This time Sam wouldn't hear the other team's coach, Mr. Boarman, grinding his teeth when he ate his Vanilla Dream Cherry Swirl. He probably should have chocolate, too. Or maybe he could close his eyes in the last inning.

I guess I'm not so sure Mr. Boarman would like another summer. Maybe he just needs a different attitude with his players. Oh, and next time Hank could play with our team. He might not be that great of a hitter, but he tells a great joke and makes us laugh hilariously.

8 At the Lake

Another summer would mean a wonder-ful fun weekend at Aunt Evy and Uncle Bud's place at the lake.

Abby and I would first need to get packed. Huge piles of suitcases and other stuff would fill the front doorsteps. It would look like we were taking the whole house along!

My pile would be big. Swimsuit, roller skates, baseball with bat and glove. All my baseball trading cards, of course. Not much, really.

Abby's pile would be huge! Mr. Cowababy, the Feline Farm Family and a ton of bubble gum packages. When he saw all the suitcases, Dad would pretend to be upset, "Abigail Moo Bovine, you've packed for a lifetime!"

All of us would need fishing poles, blow-up ducky rafts to float on and inner tubes. The

fishing poles wouldn't fit in the van, so they would have to go on top of the van. Maybe Abby could ride there, too. Just kidding, of course.

When we got there Aunt Evy would start baking up some delicious fruit pies from her own trees and gardens. We'd talk about their daily routine at the lake place. "Fishing, golfing and just relaxing." That would be the life!

Aunt Evy would tell us about the small town carnival that's held every July. They have rides and games and lots of animals to see. There's even a haunted house. I'm sure Abby would like that.

In the early evening Abby and I would help set the table for dinner. Mom, Dad, Aunt Evy and Uncle Bud would still be in the kitchen hours later, shuffling and dealing cards. Their laughter would spread as they shared stories from the past.

"MILK OR BUST"

9 Milk or Bust

If we had another summer, our Uncle Bud would take us out fishing on his boat for the afternoon.

There probably would be a ton of fish to catch. I would bring my "Lucky Champion" rod and reel set that Dad gave me on my birthday. Abby would bring her "Beginner's Choice" rod and reel set for kids. Without a doubt, this time I would catch the first fish.

Last time, in less than a hour, Abby was squealing, "I got a fish, I got a fish!" It was small, but I had to admit, it was a fish. Being a good sport I remained patient. Until the end of the day. Abby had eight fish and I only had two.

"It's okay, Corny, you can have a couple of my smaller fish if you want." Gee, thanks, Abby.

10 Swimming with the Buckeyes

The people who live next door to our aunt and uncle are the Buckeye family. They have three kids and a big dog named Chip.

If we had another summer we would throw balls in the lake and Chip would run and jump off the dock after the balls. He'd bark to make us throw them again. I don't think he would ever get tired of playing fetch. That's just a natural way of life for a dog. Kind of like me and baseball.

Our friends would take turns letting us play with the big alligator that floats. I'd pretend to be a famous alligator hunter who helps save everyone from the snarling, fanged "alligator at large."

Then we'd all line up on the dock and jump as high into the air as we could and land in the water, yelling "cannon ball!" Gus, the

oldest boy, would always make the biggest splash.

If only there was another summer, we might be able to have one more weekend at the lake with Aunt Evy and Uncle Bud.

11 Say Cheese & Goodbye

When the weekend was over, it would be time to pack up the van.

Poor Dad, his face would change color when Mom brought out that last load. Joking, he would ask Mom, "I guess we have to leave Abby behind, right?"

What a shame that would be, I thought. But somehow Dad would manage to get the van packed. He would mumble, "Not big enough. I knew we should've bought the jumbo size van instead of the small one!" Dad would be a little frustrated.

Mom would be busy saying her last goodbye to Aunt Evy in the kitchen. Her eyes would be a little watery as she would thank Aunt Evy for the wonderful time at the take. They both would be laughing about Mom's attempt to get up on the water skis. "Next time, I'll drive the

boat and let Cornelius and Abby have fun in the water."

That would be a good idea, I think. After all, Mom is getting kind of old to be doing kid's stuff.

Before leaving for home, Dad would set up the camera for a picture in front of the huge oak tree by Uncle Bud's hammock. It's a tradition. Whenever we visit, we take pictures in front of the same tree. Mom says the tree "has character." Whatever.

Aunt Evy would give us some of her homemade sugar cookies "for the road." Tired, we would pull away in the van with many great memories.

12 School Again, I Guess

If only there was another summer, we could do it all again. Baseball games under the evening lights. A fun weekend at the lake, fishing and swimming would be the best.

But back to reality. It's fall and I'm sitting in the classroom once again. Before I left home this morning Mom said: "Just smile at everyone you meet and it'll be a good day." I really think Mom reads too many books about life and raising children. But maybe not.

This morning she made an excellent breakfast for Abby and I before we left for school. We needed help to wake up for the big day. She made waffles with lots of syrup. And fresh milk, of course.

Dad helped Mom with the dishes and promised his famous spaghetti for supper.

Now that I'm here sitting in class with all

my friends, maybe school won't be so bad this year. I hope, anyway.

After all, my best friend Sam and I are in band together and it's really fun to play the trumpet. When Sam doesn't hit the snare drum just right I'm afraid to look at him. Mr. Hornsbreath doesn't like it when we laugh at somebody's mistake. He's right; it's not nice.

This morning, in front of school, I saw my other good friend, Hank. We were excited to find out that we will be in the same Spanish class. Ms. Marcias is really nice. Sometimes she bakes a Mexican meal and brings it to share with our class. Hopefully, Sam wouldn't get a noisy belly like he sometimes does. It can be really loud.

We usually get to go on a field trip to the museum in the early fall. I think the Dinosaur exhibit will still be there. Dinosaurs are my favorite.

Sam and I start hockey soon at the ice arena after school. On the weekend, we'll

BUS
OXENVIEW
ELEMENTARY

HOME SWEET HOME
SUMMER CALENDAR
FUN

have to practice on our roller skates to get in shape.

I guess I do kind of miss some parts of school. Not everything, like writing papers and taking tests, but some stuff. Art, Spanish and math are definitely my favorite subjects. I can make collages, talk in a different language and I'm pretty good at multiplication tables. Most of the time, anyway.

Lunch is great. I get to sit next to my friends. When we are done eating, we all run for the door for a quick game of touch football before the next school bell.

Back in my desk, I'm starting to feel more comfortable. Mrs. Wolfbark bellows the assignment for the next few days. "Class, I want you all to write about what you would do if you had another summer."

Smiling, I grabbed my pencil. This paper is going to be an "A." As usual, Mom was right. It'll be a good day.

About the Author

Cindy Marks has enjoyed writing short stories for newspaper and narrating them for radio. Life scheduling with a sharp eye allows her time for everything but cooking and laundry. Thankfully, when trouble comes her way, she relies on Angel(s) to keep her on track.

About the Illustrator

Steve Pickar has loved creating warm and friendly characters for as long as he can remember. His devoted base of fans is vast and consistently growing. With subtle humor and pen in hand, he has the ability to entertain both young and old.

TiaraMoon Publishing
Order Form

Name ______________________________

Address ____________________________

____

____

Phone ______________________________

If only there was...
Another Summer

Price $3.95

× Quantity (___) = __________

Shipping/Handling __________
(for one book, $2.95.
For each additional
book, $1.00.)

Total __________

Make checks payable to:

TiaraMoon Publishing
3907 Canter Glen Drive
St. Paul, Minnesota 55123